Fighting Diseases

Contents

Written by Ben Hubbard

Collins

1 A new disease

In December 2019, the world was struck by a strange new disease. It was named Covid-19. Covid-19 broke out in China, but within months, had spread across the globe. The symptoms of the disease included fever, coughing and tiredness. It was highly contagious. Tiny droplets from sneezes or coughs were enough to infect others. By December 2020, over 61 million people worldwide had been infected. To slow the spread of Covid-19, many countries went into lockdown. People were told to stay at home, and schools, offices and shops closed.

Science and medicine

Covid-19 changed modern lives. However, it is only one
of the infectious diseases that has plagued humans for
thousands of years. In the past, people didn't know how
to deal with disease. But today, advances in medicine
and knowledge have enabled us to fight back. In late
2020, scientists developed vaccines against Covid-19.
In 2021, vaccinations began all over
the world. For now, science is
winning in our ongoing
war with this disease.

2 What is a disease?

Infectious diseases are caused by germs that attack the body and make us sick. A germ is one type of tiny **organism** called a microbe. Microbes are too small to see with the naked eye, but they are everywhere: in the air, in the water, on our bodies.

Carrying germs

Not all microbes are germs, but all germs are microbes. We carry around germs all the time, including on our skin and in our noses. Most of the time, these germs don't make us ill. But they can cause tremendous harm if they invade our cells.

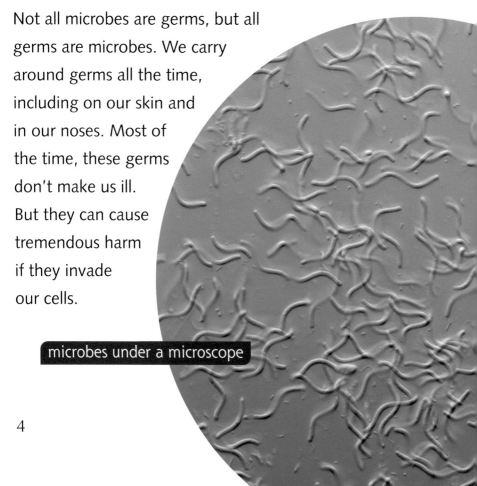

microbes under a microscope

Little animals

Humans did not know about microbes until a Dutch scientist, Antonie van Leeuwenhoek, observed them through a microscope in the 1670s. He called microbes "little animals".

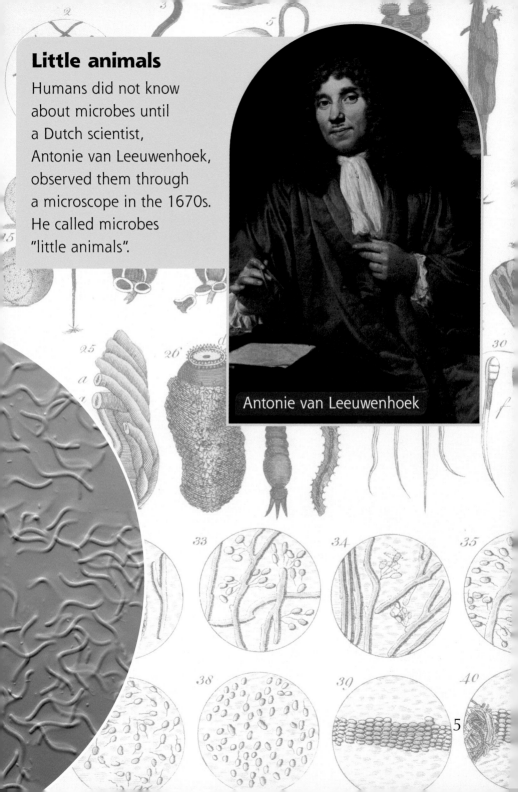

Antonie van Leeuwenhoek

3 Germ types

There are four types of germs that can make us sick: viruses, bacteria, parasites and fungi. Each one has a different way of invading our bodies.

Viruses

Viruses cause some of the world's most **contagious** diseases, such as Covid-19. They work by invading a human **cell** and making copies of themselves. These copies then invade and damage new cells, making people sick.

virus

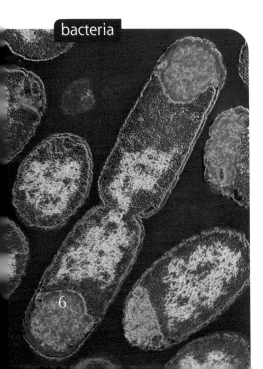

bacteria

Bacteria

Bacteria are tiny organisms that can copy themselves without invading a human cell. They multiply quickly and release **toxins** into our cells. This causes infections, such as sore throats or ear infections.

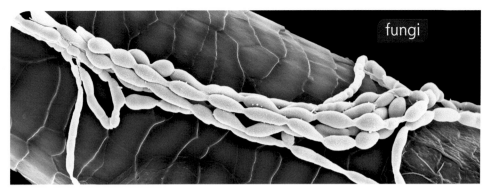
fungi

Fungi

Harmful types of fungi are plant-like organisms that live in warm, damp places. They can grow on human bodies and cause infections, such as athlete's foot which creates flaky skin and can be treated with cream.

Parasites

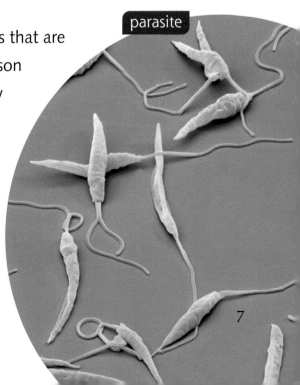
parasite

Parasites are tiny creatures that are **transmitted** from one person to another. Once in a new host body, the parasites grow and reproduce. One example, lice, look like tiny insects that can live on our heads and make us itch.

7

4 The immune system

Germs are spread in different ways.
They can enter the body through
food or drink. We can catch germs
from other people if they sneeze
or cough on us. We can even take
in germs through insect bites.
However, the body's immune system
can fight harmful germs.

tonsils and adenoids —

lymph nodes —

The immune system is the body's
natural defence against disease.
It includes skin, which stops germs
entering the body. Healthy immune
systems fight off most germs, but
sometimes, disease-causing germs
find a way inside. When this happens,
the body creates antibodies within
days to fight back. Once antibodies
are formed, they fight off the disease
and can stop it infecting the person
again in the future.

lymphatic vessels —

spleen —

appendix —

bone marrow —

diagram of the human body's immune system

9

Case study: malaria

Malaria is one of the world's oldest and deadliest diseases. It is caused by the *Plasmodium* parasite and is spread by the female Anopheles mosquito. When the mosquito bites someone infected with malaria, it picks up the parasite. It then passes it on to other people it bites.

When the *Plasmodium* parasite enters a person's body, it reproduces. New parasites then damage the victim's blood cells. The victim develops symptoms, including fever and vomiting, between seven and 30 days later.

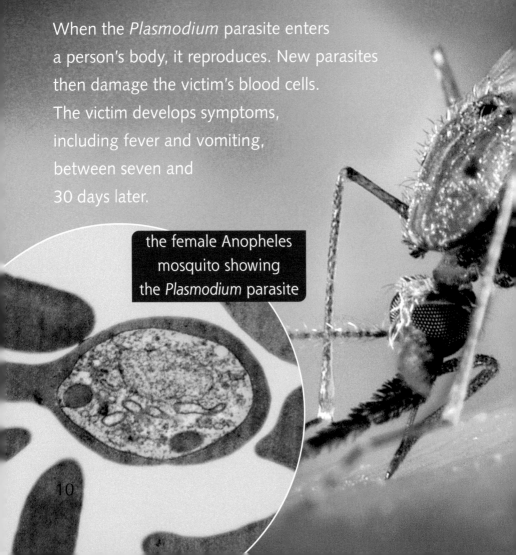

the female Anopheles mosquito showing the *Plasmodium* parasite

Ancient disease

Malaria has been infecting humans for thousands of years. Egyptian Pharaoh Tutankhamun died of the disease in 1325 BCE. Despite the development of antimalarial medication and the use of mosquito nets and repellent to avoid it, the disease still infects millions of people every year, especially in Africa.

Pharaoh Tutankhamun

5 Signs and symptoms

When somebody is infected with a disease, they show signs and symptoms. Symptoms are felt but often cannot be seen, such as extreme tiredness and muscle aches. Signs are visible, such as spots or a fever, and show a doctor what is wrong.

Spotting signs

Humans first observed microbes through a microscope in the 1670s. This enabled doctors to see the signs of disease in a patient's blood, rather than diagnosing them based on their symptoms. Since then, there have been many advances in medical instruments that help identify disease in humans.

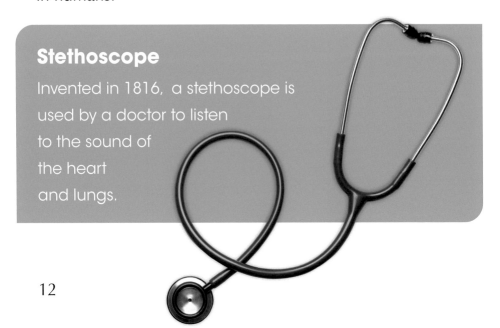

Stethoscope

Invented in 1816, a stethoscope is used by a doctor to listen to the sound of the heart and lungs.

Spirometer

A spirometer measures the amount of air a person can take into their lungs. The modern spirometer was developed in the 1800s.

Ophthalmoscope

Developed in the mid-1800s, an ophthalmoscope (say: of-thal-muh-skohp) is used for examining a patient's eye.

Sphygmomanometer

A sphygmomanometer (say: sfig-mow-muh-no-muh-tuh) fits around a patient's arm to measure their **blood pressure**. It was invented in 1896.

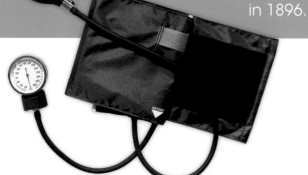

13

Case study:
the Justinian Plague

In 541CE, a terrible disease struck the city of
Constantinople (modern day Istanbul). People fell
ill with fever, diarrhoea, vomiting and pus-filled sores.
People did not know it at the time, but this was
the first-known outbreak of the plague.
It was named after Emperor Justinian I,
whose capital was based in Constantinople.

The plague is caused by the bacteria *Yersinia pestis*,
which enters the human bloodstream via the bite
of an infected flea. Fleas living on rats on
board ships probably carried the disease
to Europe from Asia and Africa.

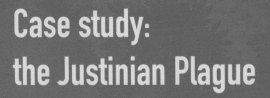

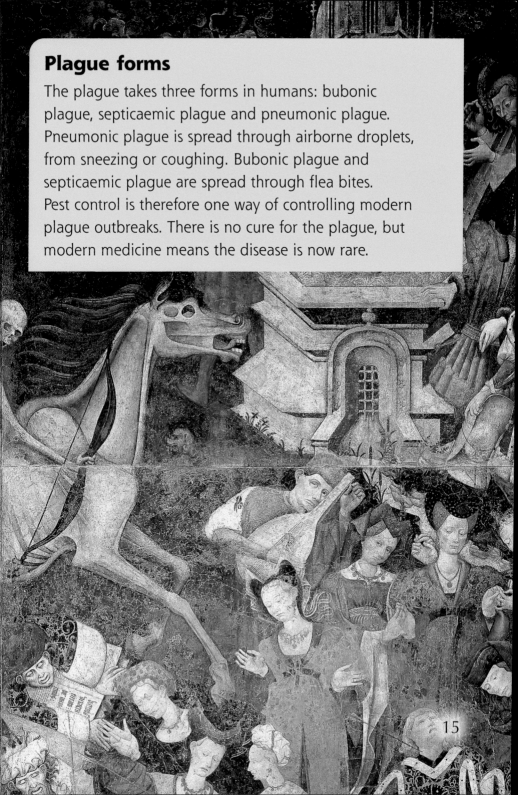

Plague forms

The plague takes three forms in humans: bubonic plague, septicaemic plague and pneumonic plague. Pneumonic plague is spread through airborne droplets, from sneezing or coughing. Bubonic plague and septicaemic plague are spread through flea bites. Pest control is therefore one way of controlling modern plague outbreaks. There is no cure for the plague, but modern medicine means the disease is now rare.

6 Epidemics and pandemics

When a large number of people are infected with a disease, it is called an epidemic. If an epidemic spreads across many countries, it is known as a pandemic. The Justinian Plague was the world's first plague pandemic.

How does it end?

Epidemics and pandemics can kill millions of people, but they do end eventually. This is often because, over time, there are fewer people for the disease to infect. Those who have had the disease have either built up antibodies to fight it or have died. In the modern world, vaccines are also developed against new diseases. Those who have been vaccinated leave the disease with fewer people to infect. It therefore slowly disappears.

Vaccines are essential in fighting a pandemic.

Masks help prevent the spread of disease during pandemics.

Case study: the Black Death

The Justinian Plague that struck Europe in the 500s did not completely disappear. Instead, it reappeared in the centuries that followed. One famous outbreak struck Europe in 1347. It was called the Black Death.

It is thought the Black Death started in Asia and was spread by rats aboard trading ships. It took its name from the black, pus-filled sores that appeared on victims' bodies. No one knew what was causing the Black Death as the importance of hygiene in preventing the spread of disease was not yet understood.

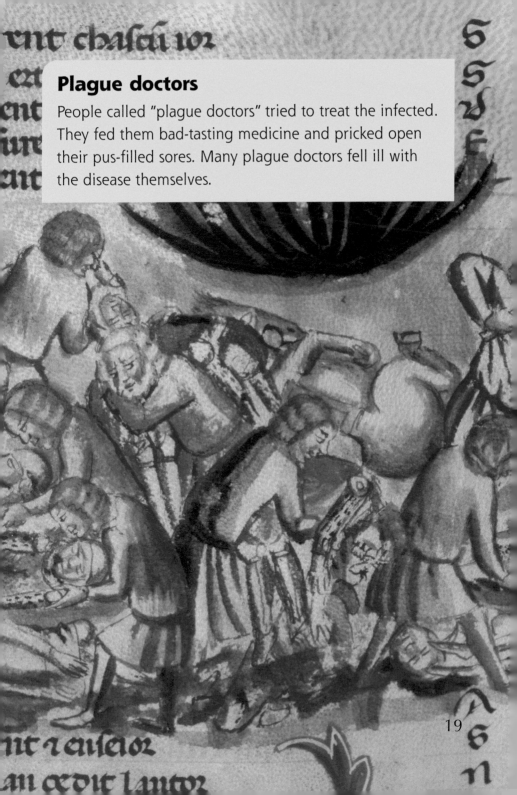

Plague doctors

People called "plague doctors" tried to treat the infected. They fed them bad-tasting medicine and pricked open their pus-filled sores. Many plague doctors fell ill with the disease themselves.

19

Quarantining

No one knew how to treat the Black Death. However, there were attempts to slow the disease. One method was to stop infected people giving the plague to others. In Venice, Italy, visiting ships had to wait in the harbour for 40 days before docking. This gave them time to recover from the disease before seeing others. This was called *quaranta giorni* ("40 days") which forms our modern word "quarantine". Today, quarantining is still an effective way of controlling pandemics.

Typhoid Mary

Typhoid Mary was the name given to a cook who infected 47 diners in New York in the early 1900s. She was discovered to be carrying the disease typhoid and was put in quarantine for three years, until she swore not to cook again.

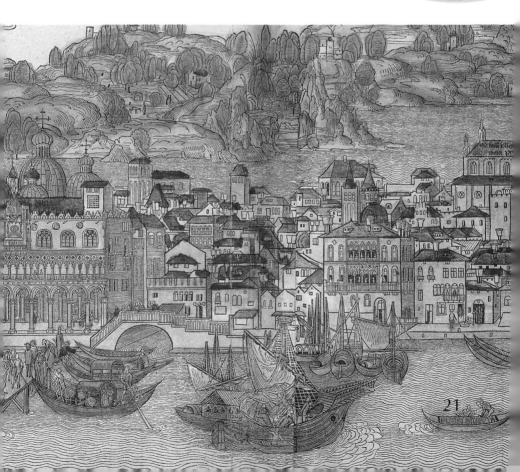

21

Case study: the Great Plague

The plague did not end in the 1300s. In 1665, another plague epidemic struck London. It spread quickly and infected thousands. We know it today as the "Great Plague".

London in the 1600s was the perfect breeding ground for the plague. It was an overcrowded, filthy city where people threw their waste onto the street. This attracted rats which carried the pneumonic plague and septicaemic plague. But the bubonic plague spread even faster, by people sneezing on each other.

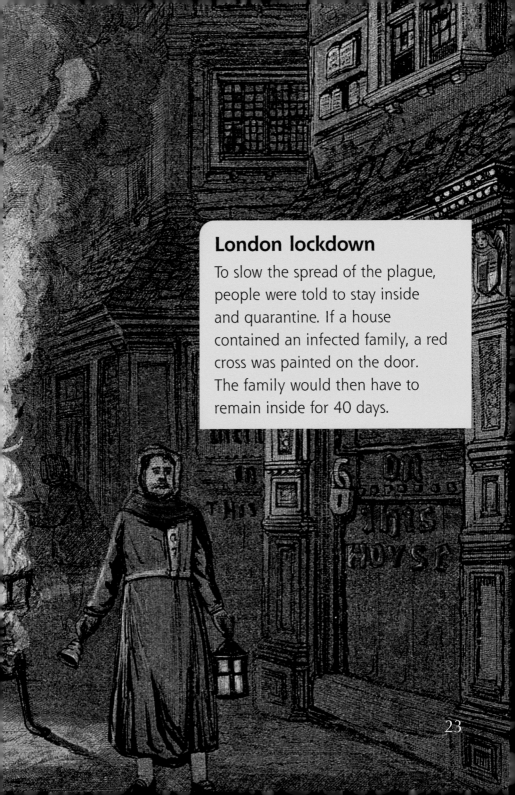

London lockdown

To slow the spread of the plague, people were told to stay inside and quarantine. If a house contained an infected family, a red cross was painted on the door. The family would then have to remain inside for 40 days.

Masks and miasma

In the 1600s, no one realised that airborne droplets in sneezes could spread the Great Plague. By wearing masks, the spread of the disease could have been slowed. Some masks were actually worn by plague doctors.

However, these were not to protect against sneezing, but instead, "bad air". This bad air, called miasma, was wrongly believed to be spreading the plague. Londoners were told to burn fires to ward miasma away.

masks to fight disease from different times

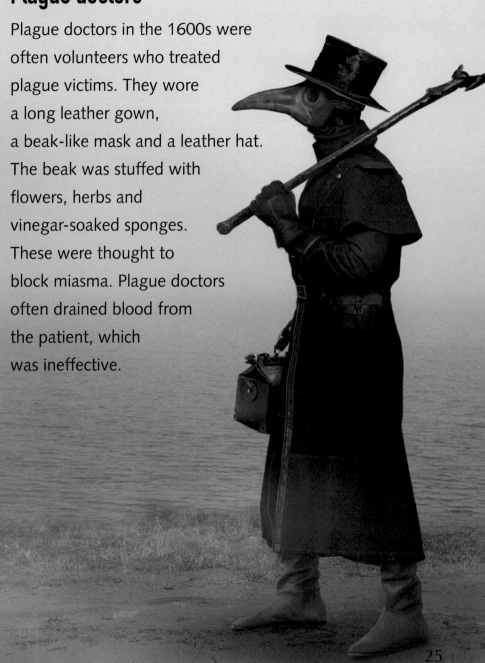

Plague doctors

Plague doctors in the 1600s were
often volunteers who treated
plague victims. They wore
a long leather gown,
a beak-like mask and a leather hat.
The beak was stuffed with
flowers, herbs and
vinegar-soaked sponges.
These were thought to
block miasma. Plague doctors
often drained blood from
the patient, which
was ineffective.

Case study: smallpox

For thousands of years, the smallpox virus was one of the deadliest diseases in the world. Its symptoms included fever and severe headaches. It also caused red sores to erupt on the face and body which left disfiguring pockmarks and scars.

Smallpox outbreaks began in the ancient world, but reappeared in the 500s, 600s and 1000s. In the 1500s, Europeans brought the disease to new countries. The Aztec civilisation of Central America was nearly wiped out by smallpox brought by Spanish invaders. First Nations Australians suffered a similar fate in the 1800s, when European settlers brought smallpox to Australia.

Ali Maow Maalin developed smallpox on 26 October 1977. He was the last case of smallpox.

Elizabeth I

English Queen Elizabeth I was heavily pockmarked after catching smallpox. To conceal her pockmarks, Elizabeth wore a thick face paint. However, this face paint contained lead and probably contributed to her early death.

7 The first vaccine

For centuries, outbreaks of smallpox ravaged the world. The only safe people were those who had already had smallpox and were now immune. Then, in Turkey in the 1700s, doctors found that giving healthy people a small dose of smallpox actually made them **immune** to the disease.

Jenner's jab

In 1796, English doctor Edward Jenner used the immunity theory from Turkey to develop the first smallpox vaccine. Jenner gave his patients a dose of cowpox, a similar disease to smallpox, but milder. It made the patients immune to smallpox. Jenner developed this into a vaccine. In 1980, the World Health Organisation used Jenner's vaccine to rid the world of smallpox altogether.

Edward Jenner

Case study: tuberculosis

Tuberculosis (also called "TB") is an ancient disease that attacks a person's lungs. It is also known as consumption, because it appears to consume its victims. Those infected with TB become thin and pale, and cough up blood.

Tuberculosis outbreaks have been occurring for thousands of years. However, the worst modern TB pandemics occurred between 1600 and 1800. During this time, the disease was responsible for 25 per cent of all European deaths. The worst affected areas were overcrowded city **slums**.

John Keats, a famous poet, died of tuberculosis in 1821.

Until the late 1800s, not much could be done for people infected with TB. Some of the strange treatments included draining blood and horse-riding. In the United States, it was wrongly thought people that had died of TB could come back as vampires and infect others.

a city slum, London, around 1840

8 Science and sanatoriums

In 1882, a German doctor, Robert Koch, discovered that TB was caused by the bacterium *Mycobacterium tuberculosis*. This was a major breakthrough because it showed that TB was an infectious disease. Someone infected with TB could therefore infect others by sneezing or coughing on them.

Robert Koch

Country quarantine

In the late 1800s, hospitals called sanatoriums were built in the countryside to quarantine TB sufferers. It gave them a chance to fight the disease somewhere with clean air and healthy food. The sanatoriums were closed when a TB vaccine was developed. TB still continues to infect people today, although antibiotic treatment is available.

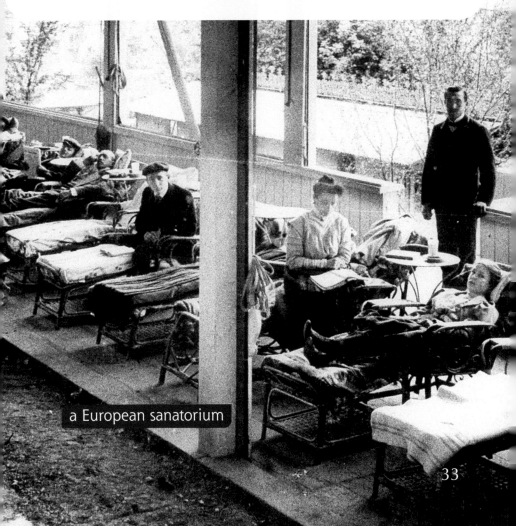

a European sanatorium

Case study: cholera

Cholera, which is caused by the *Vibrio cholerae* bacterium, was considered a minor disease before the 1800s. But in 1817, there was a large cholera outbreak in India. This quickly spread and caused seven pandemics over the next hundred years.

Cholera victims experienced vomiting, diarrhoea and dehydration. No one knew what was causing the disease. As cholera arrived in Russia and Europe in the 1830s, governments tried to slow its spread. In Russia, the army destroyed bridges to stop infected people entering the cites.

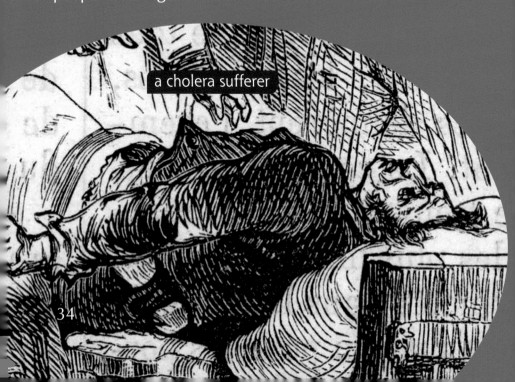

a cholera sufferer

City cholera

There was a link between cholera and unclean, overcrowded areas. The disease thrived in city slums which were often home to large **immigrant** populations. For this reason, foreigners and immigrants were often unfairly blamed for the disease.

"WATER! WATER! EVERYWHERE;
AND NOT A DROP TO DRINK."

Coleridge.

9 Advances in science

No one was sure what was causing the spread of cholera in the 1800s. An English doctor, John Snow, thought the disease was connected to dirty water. In London, many people collected their drinking water from the Broad Street water pump. In 1854, Snow had the pump cut off and cholera cases dropped. It was then found that sewage was leaking into the pump water.

a newspaper cartoon of the Broad Street water pump

John Snow

John Snow's map of 19th Century London

Studying disease

Snow's research was a major breakthrough in the fight against cholera. He became one of the founders of epidemiology – the study of disease in populations. By building sewers and providing clean drinking water, the disease was wiped out in many countries. However, it still persists in some countries today, where rehydration treatment is needed.

Case study: Spanish flu

Influenza is an infectious virus which strikes every winter. Most people survive the "flu", but in 1918, an influenza outbreak became the worst pandemic since the Black Death. It was called the Spanish flu.

No one is sure where the 1918 influenza outbreak first emerged. In the USA, it spread in an army training camp. Returning soldiers from the First World War spread the disease around the world. Newspapers reporting its outbreak in Spain gave the disease its name. It quickly spread throughout the world and infected over 500 million people.

Spanish flu attacked in two waves: one mild and one severe. There was no vaccine or drugs to treat Spanish flu. However, many people had developed immunity by April 1920 and the pandemic came to an end.

10 Antibiotics

Alexander Fleming was a Scottish doctor who worked in army hospitals during the First World War. He saw the devastation that Spanish flu caused. He also observed many soldiers dying of wounds infected with bacteria. At the time, there was no way of treating these wounds. After the war, Fleming decided to find a way to cure infections.

Accidental antibiotic

Fleming discovered a cure by accident. He left out a dish filled with bacteria which became covered in mould. This mould, called *Penicillium*, had killed the bacteria. Fleming developed the mould into the world's first antibiotic, penicillin. Antibiotics stop microbes, such as bacteria, growing and reproducing. Fleming's discovery was a major breakthrough which has saved countless lives from many dangerous forms of bacteria.

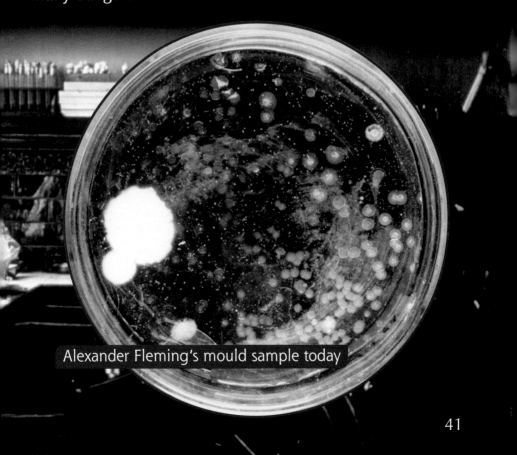

Alexander Fleming's mould sample today

11 Science saves

Today, we have science to thank for our success against the spread of disease. In the past, diseases swept across the world, killing millions. No one knew how to stop or even slow their spread. It was only with the development of the microscope that diseases could be identified. Tiny microbes were invading our bodies and making us sick.

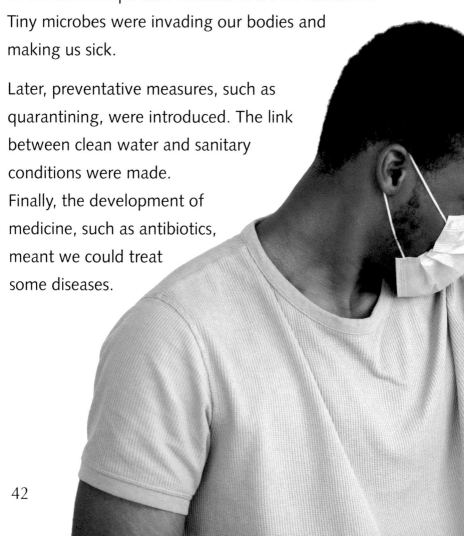

Later, preventative measures, such as quarantining, were introduced. The link between clean water and sanitary conditions were made. Finally, the development of medicine, such as antibiotics, meant we could treat some diseases.

These medicines are vital in the fight against diseases that are still with us, such as tuberculosis and sepsis. Scientific research into disease also enabled the rollout of vaccines and antiviral medication against Covid-19 in 2021.

It is these medicines that have prevented countless deaths and allowed us to live with the modern diseases of our time.

Glossary

blood pressure the pressure at which the heart pushes blood around the body

cell the smallest structure in an organism

contagious when a disease is able to spread

immigrant a person who moves permanently to a foreign country

immune protected against a disease

organism a living thing, such as an animal, plant or germ

slums crowded, run-down areas of a city

transmitted passed on from one person to another

toxins poisons that come from plants or animals

Index

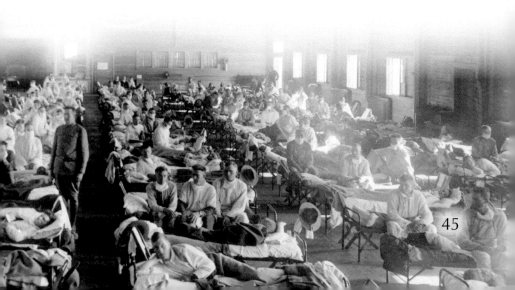

Diseases

Disease	Caused by ...	Avoided with ...
malaria	parasite	mosquito nets and repellent
plague	bacteria	quarantine, pest control
smallpox	virus	vaccination
tuberculosis	bacteria	vaccination
cholera	bacteria	clean water
Spanish flu	virus	quarantine
Covid-19	virus	social distancing, quarantine and vaccination

Treatment ...	Rare or common now?
antimalarial medication for prevention and treatment	common
antibiotics	rare
no cure after infection, but people sometimes recovered	eliminated
antibiotics	common
no cure, but treatable with rehydration solution	rare
no cure	rare
no cure, but symptoms can be treated with antiviral medication	common

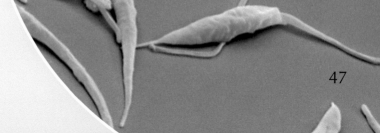

 Ideas for reading

Written by Gill Matthews
Primary Literacy Consultant

Reading objectives:
- check that the text makes sense to them, discuss their understanding and explain the meaning of words in context
- ask questions to improve their understanding of a text
- identify main ideas drawn from more than one paragraph and summarise these

Spoken language objectives:
- ask relevant questions to extend their understanding and knowledge
- use spoken language to develop understanding through speculating, hypothesising, imagining and exploring ideas
- participate in discussions, presentations, performances, role play, improvisations and debates

Curriculum links: Citizenship – Developing a healthy, safer lifestyle

Interest words: invading, introduced, enabled, prevented

Resources: IT

Build a context for reading
- Ask children to look at the front cover of the book and to read the title. Discuss what diseases they are aware of. Ask what they think the image on the cover is showing, and how these methods might be helping to fight diseases.
- Read the back-cover blurb. Discuss what children think they might find out from the book.
- Discuss what kind of book children think this is. Ask what features they expect it to have. Give them time to skim the book to find the contents, glossary and index. Explore children's knowledge of these features, including their purpose and how they are organised.

Understand and apply reading strategies
- Read pp2–3 aloud. Explore children's knowledge of Covid-19, being aware of any sensitive situations that might exist. Ask how they think the fight against Covid-19 was different from the fights against previous diseases.